YORK
THEN & NOW

IN COLOUR

PAUL CHRYSTAL

COLOUR PHOTOGRAPHY BY MARK SUNDERLAND

The History Press

For Joe Dickinson and Melvyn Browne

'There is abundance of good company here, and abundance of good families live here, for the sake of the good company and cheap living; a man converses here with all the world as effectually as at London.'

Daniel Defoe, *A Tour Thro' The Whole Island of Great Britain* (1724)

First published 2010
Reprinted 2015

The History Press
The Mill, Brimscombe Port
Stroud, Gloucestershire, GL5 2QG
www.thehistorypress.co.uk

British Library Cataloguing in Publication Data.
A catalogue record for this book is available from the British Library.

ISBN 978 0 7524 5735 2

Typesetting and origination by The History Press
Printed in China

CONTENTS

Acknowledgements   5

Introduction   7

1.   Railways, Trams and Barges   9

2.   Rivers and Bridges   21

3.   Pubs, Hotels and a Cinema   27

4.   Shops, Markets and Factories   35

5.   Bar Walls, Bars and Clifford's Tower   49

6.   York Minster and Other Places of Religion   57

7.   York People and Special Occasions   61

8.   A Tour Around York   69

ACKNOWLEDGEMENTS

Thanks go to the following for their help and advice, and for being so generous with their photographs and postcards; the book would be much diminished without them: Melvyn Browne; Anne Chrystal; Cross of York, Newgate Market (p.26); Joe Dickinson; East Coast, York railway station (p. 13); Keith and Karen Hyman, former Sheriff and Lady Sheriff of York; Hilary King; Rupert Matthews (p.86). Any errors that remain are mine.

More of Mark Sunderland's work can be found at
www.marksunderland.com

ST MICHAEL-LE-BELFRY (below) with the Minster in the background, and a panoramic view of York from Clifford's Tower (above). In any other city St Michael-le-Belfry would be a jewel in their crown; in York it is indeed a jewel but, despite its beauty, seems forever in the shadow of the Minster. So it's good to see the roles reversed for a change. The interior is largely Tudor, having been rebuilt in 1536; its name is due to its proximity to the Minster bell tower. Guy Fawkes was baptised here on 16 April 1570.

INTRODUCTION

York is one of those rare English cities which has been touched by and which, in turn, has influenced nearly every major period of British history.

King George VI put it well when he said, 'The history of York is the history of England.' Roman and Viking occupation, the Norman Conquest, Reformation, Pilgrimage of Grace, Gunpowder Plot, Council in the North and the English Civil War, the birth of the railways and the confectionary industry, Victorian social reform, the world wars – York has played a significant part in all of these.

In addition to the most extensive surviving city walls in Britain and the largest Gothic cathedral north of Milan, it can boast some of the most attractive medieval streets in Europe and best-preserved buildings dating from the early 1300s right through to the Georgian age of elegance, when York was regarded as the northern capital of gentility and style.

York Then & Now captures this pageant through a unique juxtaposing of old photographs, dating from the dawn of photography, with contemporary pictures. Together they show vividly how York was and how it is today, they show what has changed, what remains the same, and what has gone for good. Add to this the incisive and informative captions and you have a book which can be dipped into at random or read as an engaging history of this intriguing city and its people.

It provides readers – be they visitor, local resident or nostalgic émigré – with a fascinating at-a-glance glimpse of York's people, special occasions, buildings, shops, factories, streets, railways, rivers and bridges, placing them in historical and contemporary context.

York can also boast an impressive cast of fascinating characters who have left their mark on the city: William the Conqueror and many other kings and queens of England after him, not least Charles I during the Civil War; Guy Fawkes (born here); Dick Turpin (executed here); Margaret Clitherow (martyred here); George Hudson (railway king), Benjamin Seebohm Rowntree (Quaker social reformer); Joseph Rowntree and Joseph Terry (confectionary and chocolate manufacturers); Joseph Hansom (inventor of the eponymous cab) and W.H. Auden – all make cameo appearances here.

Minster, bars (medieval gates) and walls apart, York is rightly famous for its timber-framed buildings, narrow streets and snickelways: Shambles and Stonegate are world famous – Mad Alice Lane, Pope's Head Alley and Mucky Peg Lane deserve to be. The elegant Assembly Rooms, medieval Merchant Adventurer's

Hall, thirteenth-century Lady Row and England's first mansion house are all pictured here along with some fine, ancient, unspoiled pubs and a host of beautiful churches.

The railway industry and chocolate manufacturing which York pioneered have left their indelible marks on the city; the effects of the world wars through Zeppelin bombings and the 1942 Baedeker raid are also there to see.

The grandeur of the city today has been magnificently captured through the photography of Mark Sunderland – a fine testament to what remains today one of the finest cities in Europe. In addition I would like to thank Joe Dickinson and Melvyn Browne for the help and information they have freely given, and for access to their fantastic collections of postcards, covering every imaginable aspect of York.

The content of the book is obviously limited by space and it is hoped that a second volume will follow, covering such glaring omissions as St Mary's Abbey, King's Manor, Lendal Bridge and other towers, the many museums, Whip-Ma-Whop-Ma-Gate, Merchant Taylor's Hall, Fairfax House, the Treasurer's House, the Council in the North and the Mystery Plays, venerable schools and more ancient streets with their houses, taverns, shops and churches.

Paul Chrystal, 2010

1

RAILWAYS, TRAMS
AND BARGES

(Courtesy of Melvyn Browne)

Interior of York Station.

THE BREATHTAKING SWEEP of York railway station's roof in 1904. At 800ft long and 234ft wide this is one of the most spectacular examples of railway architecture in the world, rightly and famously described by one of the North Eastern Railway shareholders at its opening in 1877 as 'A splendid monument of extravagance'. The railway king, George Hudson, was prominent in York's development as a major railway city; his advice to George Stephenson was to make it a hub: 'Mak all t'railways cum t'York.'

The first train left York for South Milford in 1839. The first London service was in 1840 via Derby or Birmingham and took between ten and eleven hours. In 1841, the industry in York employed forty-one people, this rose to 513 by 1851 (390 of whom were from out of town bringing 537 dependents), and by the end of the century NER employed 5,500 workers in York, about half in the carriage works. In the 1850s the railway replaced the five or so stagecoaches per day between London and York which started in 1703 (carrying 24,000 passengers per year, six per coach, and taking between four and six days depending on the weather) with thirteen trains carrying 341,000 passengers. The fare to London via Grantham in 1882 was 33s 4d (first class), 25s 4d (second class – equal to about one week's wages for a semi-skilled man) and 15s 8d (third class). By 1888 there were 294 trains arriving at the station each day: this all led to a marked rise in York's tourist industry; it also revolutionised communications. By the mid-1860s York had two daily postal deliveries; a letter posted in London before noon was delivered in York later the same evening! York's main post office, in Lendal, was built in 1884. The emerging confectionary industry with Rowntrees, Terry's and Craven's also benefited enormously from the railways.

(Courtesy of Joe Dickinson)

ABOVE: THIS PICTURE shows railway workers mingling with some extremely well-dressed gentlemen and ladies on Queen Street bridge (built in 1880) during the York Railway Strike of 1911. Around 18 August, the general secretary of the Amalgamated Society of Railway Servants announced the beginning of the first national railway strike with the words 'War is declared, the men are being called out'. It was in support of the riotous (and for some, fatal) Liverpool Transport Strike, when troops were deployed to attack the strikers. Queen Street was originally called Thief Lane and it was once traversed by a level crossing. The less dramatic modern photograph (below) shows that the road has been considerably widened and the sidings replaced by the car park.

YORK RAILWAY STATION. This is in fact York's third station. The first was a temporary wooden building on Queen Street outside the walls, opened in 1839 by the York & North Midland Railway on the site of the Dominican Friary. In 1841 it was succeeded, within the walls, by what is now called the old York railway station (demolished in 1966). The King of Saxony and Charles Dickens were amongst travellers arriving here. Because through trains between London and Newcastle needed to reverse out of the station in order to continue their journey, a new station was built outside the walls. This is the present station, designed by the NER architects Thomas Prosser and William Peachey; it opened in 1877, costing £400,000 on the site of a Roman cemetery. It had thirteen platforms and was at that time the largest station in the world: the main platform is 500ft long. As part of the new station project, the Royal Station Hotel (now The Royal York Hotel), designed by Peachey, opened in 1878.

(Courtesy of Joe Dickinson)

ABOVE: WITH THE Minster towering in the background, this dramatic shot from the 1960s shows the excitement generated by the Southern Railways steam locomotive crossing Scarborough Bridge over the River Ouse. The bridge is a T-girder, which was built in twelve weeks in 1845 to the design of Robert Stephenson and cost £3,918 1*d*. It catered for foot and rail. Originally, pedestrians had to walk between the two tracks, but the entrance was later bricked up and a safer footpath constructed. A bridge of similar construction in Chester collapsed in 1847. The picture below shows the 1875 reconstruction.

(Courtesy of Joe Dickinson)

ABOVE: SOME OF damage visited on platform 1 by the Luftwaffe on 28 April 1942 in retaliation for the RAF's destruction of Lübeck and Rostock. The raids on York, Norwich, Bath, Canterbury and Exeter became known as the Baedeker Raids because Göring's staff allegedly used the famous travel guide to select their Vergeltungsangriffe (retaliatory) targets – namely three-star English cities. Seventy German bombers, largely unopposed, bombed the city for two hours: eighty-six people died, including fourteen children, and ninety-eight were seriously injured (not including undisclosed army and RAF fatalities). Over 9,500 houses (30 per cent of the city's stock) were damaged or destroyed, leaving 2,000 people homeless, as well as the Guildhall and St Martin le Grand Church. The Bar Convent School collapsed, killing five nuns including the headmistress, Mother Vincent. The following day the *Daily Mail* reported: 'The gates of York still stand high, like the spirit of its people who, after nearly two hours of intense bombing and machine-gunning, were clearing up today.' The plaque is in honour of station foreman, William Milner, who died in the raid while entering a burning building to get medical supplies. His body was found still holding the box. He was posthumously awarded the King's Commendation for Gallantry.

13

ABOVE: AN ARTIST'S impression of a tram being hauled up Micklegate Hill (*see* p. 18) in 1905. St Martin-cum-Gregory Church can be seen here, although it is now no longer used for church services. It was mentioned in the Domesday Book. Much of the building is fourteenth and fifteenth century and the tower plinth is made from stone pillaged from the Roman Temple of Mithras. The tower itself dates from 1844. A butter market thrived here until 1838 and, at its peak, butter exports from York amounted to 80,000 firkins. The adverts on the tram are for Reckitts Blue (a laundry whitener) and Zebra grate polish. The rules at the bottom read 'Will Ladies Remain Seated When Hill Is Reached – Gentlemen Should Get Out and Wait at the Top'.

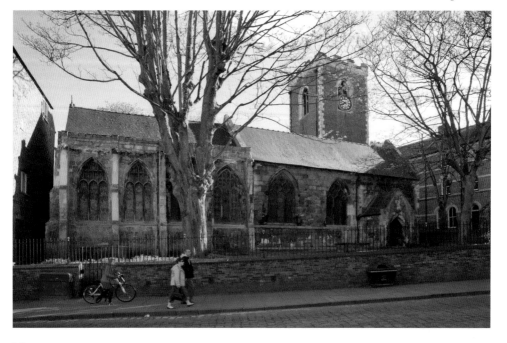

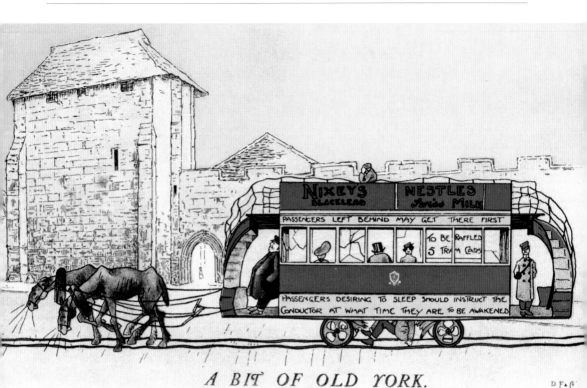

A BIT OF OLD YORK.

D.F.C

ABOVE: AN ARTIST'S impression of a horse-drawn tram passing the Fishergate Postern Tower in 1905. Buildings adjoining the postern (a back door allowing access to the walls) were destroyed in a 1489 riot. The tower was built in 1505 and originally called Edward's Tower. A lavatory projecting from the tower discharged into the adjacent King's Pool. Dick Turpin's grave is nearby in the garden on the site of St George's Church. He was executed on 7 April 1739, after spending time in a cell which can still be seen in the Debtors' Prison in the Castle Museum. The adverts on this one are for Nixeys Black Lead and Nestlé's Swiss Milk. Below you can see the Fishergate Postern Tower as it is today.

(Author's collection)

(Courtesy of Joe Dickinson)

ABOVE: SURVEYING THE laying of electric tram lines in 1910 under the city walls through the 1876 breach – to take over from horse-drawn trams. In 1900 there were eleven such trams drawn by a pool of thirty-three horses. The lines were all taken up again in 1935 as car use increased. The last tram journey from Nessgate, on Saturday 16 November, was witnessed by large crowds gathered at midnight to watch the Lord Mayor and Inspector J. Stewart – the driver of the very first service – drive York trams into oblivion. With hindsight, perhaps this was slightly ill-advised when you consider today's traffic congestion. The electrification cost £89,741, with over eight miles of track laid. The former Railway Offices in the background are now the Cedar Court Grand Hotel & Spa, which opened in May 2010.

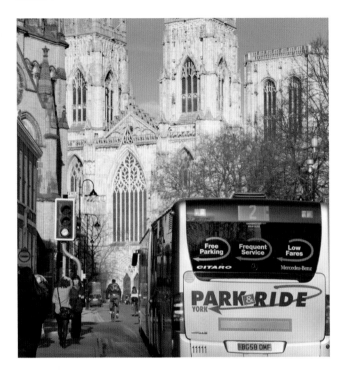

BELOW: A NUMBER 18 tram comes down Duncombe Place from the Minster as a horse-drawn bus passes it going in the other direction. A horse and cart and a hand cart can also be seen. St Wilfrid's Church is on the left along with the tastefully restored Red House; the pub on the right is now Thomas', named after Thomas Erridge – Sherriff of York in 1832 – and originaly called the Erridge Royal Hotel. Duncombe Place was built between 1860 and 1864 by demolishing buildings on the corner of Blake Street and Lop Lane. The first day of the tram service, 20 January 1910, saw 6,786 passengers carried, with fares totalling £35 18s 5d – as the fare was 2d there must have been quite a few fare dodgers.

(Courtesy of Joe Dickinson)

THREE AGES OF public transport. The older of the two photographs, dating from 1906, shows the horse-drawn bus going up Micklegate Hill past the 'Family & Commercial Hotel', followed by a brewer's dray. The new City of York Tramways (founded in 1879) tram is going between Nessgate and Fulford. Going up Micklegate Hill required three horses, a trace horse (seen on the right) being held in reserve to provide additional horse power should one of the other two not make it up. A horse with the name of Dobbin reputedly did the job for many years, making his own way back down the hill to his post outside the post office until next required. Modern horse power is shown in the modern photograph below.

18

(Courtesy of Melvyn Browne)

ABOVE: THE PROUD crew of number 27 tram, probably taken during the First World War when women were permitted to do traditional 'men's work'. Rail cars (as trams were technically called) plied between Fulford and South Bank; Fulford and Acomb; Haxby Road and South Bank; and Haxby Road and Acomb – and vice versa on a ten-minute service between 8 a.m. and 10.45 p.m., plus works specials; 2-10 p.m. on Sundays. The universal fare was 2*d* per journey. Today, long buses snake their way in and out of the walls in an incongruous meeting of old and new.

(Courtesy of Melvyn Browne)

ABOVE: BARGES LOADING up with coal and sand on the River Foss at J.H. Walker & Co., Layerthorpe Bridge, in the early 1950s. Walkers provided all sorts of domestic and steam coal, as well as anthracite washed nuts, Welsh smokeless steam coal, Glasshoughton furnace coke and coke nuts. The Foss was continually dredged – the Reklaw dredger can be seen to the right of the barge. The gasometers and chimneys in the background were owned by York Gas Company – gas being first supplied in 1824, helping to keep York comparatively smoke free. The modern photograph shows how the area has been totally redeveloped as the home of light industry and retail units.

2

RIVERS
AND BRIDGES

THE RIVER OUSE from Lendal Bridge, looking up to Ouse Bridge with the Guildhall and *Yorkshire Herald* newspaper offices on the left. The present Ouse Bridge was built between 1810 and 1821 (a previous one was washed away by floods and ice in 1564). A wooden bridge before that, built in AD 850, collapsed with hundreds of people on it, who had gathered to welcome Archbishop William back to the city in 1154 from Sicily after his reinstatement. William made the sign of the cross on seeing the calamity, no one died and the event was immediately declared a miracle. The main pleasure boat companies were Hill's at Lendal Bridge and Air's at Ouse Bridge. Hill's ran daily services to Poppleton and the Archbishop's Palace; the return fare in 1929 was 1s, children 6d. The family ran the business until November 1971. The subterranean Common Hall Lane passes under the Guildhall (opened in 1459 and usually called Common Hall) to a jetty on the river and was originally a continuation of Stonegate. The Guildhall was extensively damaged during the 1942 Baedeker Raid and was subsequently rebuilt. *(Author's collection)*

(Courtesy of Joe Dickinson)

LENDAL BRIDGE OPENED in 1863 after the first bridge (designed prophetically by an engineer called Dredge) collapsed, killing five men. The bridge replaced a ferry. John Leeman was the last ferryman – he received £15 and a horse and cart in compensation. The view above looks toward the Railway Offices(now the Cedar Court Grand Hotel & Spa) in Station Road, with Tanner Row on the left and the Maltings pub, formerly known as The Lendal; John J. Hunt's brewery offices are next door. The next row has since been replaced by the older of the two Aviva Insurance (formerly Norwich Union) buildings on the corner of Rougier Street.

MARYGATE LANDING. The River Ouse was crucial to York from earliest times, right through the Roman and Viking occupations and the Middle Ages, making York an important port. Evidence of Irish and German boats in the city dates from around 1125. The image below looks down the Ouse at Marygate Landing toward Lendal Bridge with the Water Tower that used to serve St Mary's Abbey. The two sailing barges are unloading what is probably coal onto the horse and cart for onward delivery. Today the commercial river traffic has been replaced by pleasure boats and canoes and the river banks provide pleasant riverside walks and a cycle route to Selby.

(Courtesy of Melvyn Browne)

(Courtesy of Melvyn Browne)

ABOVE: SKATING ON the Ouse during freezing early twentieth-century conditions; the ice is said to have been up to 12ft thick at times. Apart from the skating, horse chestnut sellers bravely set up hot braziers and stalls on the ice, and there were even horse races between the Tower and Marygate in 1740 and football matches in 1607. In 1740, Thomas Gent set up his printing press on the ice, producing a leaflet to celebrate the event. Terry's old factory can be seen smoking away on the right in Clementhorpe, before the move to Bishopthorpe. The photo was taken from the Ouse Bridge looking toward Skeldergate Bridge. The original wooden twelfth-century Ouse Bridge was populated with up to fifty buildings, including St William's Chapel, a prison and a hospital. The modern photograph (below) shows how the riverside has been successfully redeveloped.

ABOVE: A SPECTACULAR shot of Skeldergate Bridge being opened in the 1930s. The castle-like building is still there. It was a toll house and the cost to cross it, up to 1914, was ½*d*. Opposite, in St George's Fields, was the York ducking stool – for scoundrels and women who sold short measures or bad beer, and 'scolds and flyters'. The gallows nearby attracted large crowds, some of whom came by special train excursions as late as 1862. The bridge was started in 1875 and opened in 1881 at a cost of £56,000 – 40 per cent over budget. It was a toll bridge until 1914. The opening mechanism has since been immobilised; the bridge was strengthened in 1938.

(Courtesy of Melvyn Browne)

ABOVE: A SPLENDID white whale, 12ft-long and weighing 50 stone, which was spotted in the Ouse at Cawood in 1905 by salmon fisherman Tom Smith and promptly shot by him. It was paraded through the streets and proudly displayed on a W. Green of Cawood coal merchant rulley here in the yard of the Pack Horse pub in Micklegate (demolished 1957). Stories regarding its fate vary: some say it was cut up and distributed to local fishmongers; others maintain that it was presented to York Philosophical Society Museum. Seals are also sometimes seen in the Ouse. The most famous was Sammy, who lived in Linton Lock in 2002 for months; the most recent was spotted in May 2010 near Bishopthorpe Palace. Today's fishmongers in Newgate Market may not have whale for sale, but they're extremely busy all the same.

3

PUBS, HOTELS
AND A CINEMA

THE ELECTRIC THEATRE, Fossgate was one of six cinemas operating in York by 1929. It was opened in 1911 and you went in through an entrance beneath the screen; from 1951 it was known as the Scala, but it closed in 1957 and became MacDonald's furniture shop, the exterior still beautifully preserved today. Locally it was known as the 'Flea Bin' – and a visit meant a 'laugh and scratch'. Admission on Saturday afternoon was 4*d* – or a clean jam jar (an early example of recycling). By 1940 you could choose from: The Picture House in Coney Street (where Boots now is); the Tower in New Street (so small it only had four rows in the balcony); St George's (next to Fairfax House); the Electric; the Regent (Acomb); the Grand (Clarence Street); the Art-Deco Odeon in Blossom Street and the Art-Deco Clifton; and the Rialto, which promoted itself as offering 'World Famous artists of Radio, Stage, Screen and Concert Platform; World Famous Orchestras [and] World famous Films'. The Clifton (cinema and ballroom) was the first to have an organ that rose in front of the screen; its first film was *Sabu the Elephant Boy*.

ABOVE: THE WHITE Swan Hotel. On the corner of Pavement and Coppergate the upper storeys of this magnificent building have unfortunately lain empty for many years. It was occupied for a while by the York Peace Collective. The White Swan Hotel was, in 1974, the original venue for York Book Fair, which has grown into the largest rare, antiquarian and out-of-print book fair in the UK and is now held at the Knavesmire over two days. Two hundred booksellers offer a massive range of books, maps and prints for up to tens of thousands of pounds. The ground floor is now Jessops, while Fosters, the corn seed and coal merchants next door, is now the wonderful Duttons for Buttons.

(Courtesy of Joe Dickinson)

(Courtesy of Joe Dickinson)

ABOVE: BUILT ON the site of the York Tavern in 1770, Harker's York Hotel was named after a butler who worked at the tavern. It was pulled down in 1928 so that St Helen's Square could be widened. Harker's then decamped to Dringhouses; a 1929 advertisement claimed it to be 'The best and most up to date hotel in the city'. The name lives on in the Square though: Harker's Bar now occupies the grand Yorkshire Insurance Company building which opened in 1924. Betty's famous tea rooms (below) have occupied the old Harker's site since 1937. In 1936 the founder, Frederick Belmont, travelled on the maiden voyage of the *Queen Mary*. He was so impressed that he commissioned the ship's designers to turn what had been an old furniture shop into his most sophisticated tea rooms – and that's what you get in the art-deco upstairs function room. St Helen's Church – another gem – can be seen in the background.

29

(Courtesy of Joe Dickinson)

THE GOLDEN FLEECE Hotel still survives (with its impressive golden sheep hanging above the door) on Pavement – as does the fifteenth-century timber-framed Tudor mansion in the centre, once the home of Thomas Herbert, Bart, born there in 1606. To the right in the picture above is Rowntrees shop; members of the family lived above the shop. To the left of the photo you can just see the impressive coat of arms for the Merchant Adventurers' Company. The pub is reputedly haunted, home to no fewer than seven ghosts. Earliest mention is in the City Archive of 1503; it originally belonged to The Merchant Adventurers, who named it to celebrate their thriving woollen trade. In 1702, John Peckett, the Lord Mayor, owned it. The building has no foundations, which accounts in part for its lopsidedness.

(Author's collection)

THE BLACK SWAN in Peasholme Green; former coaching station, haunted, and also known as the 'Mucky Duck', it is one of the oldest licensed houses in York. However, originally it wasn't a pub but the home of William Bowes, former sheriff, mayor and MP between 1417 and 1428. It still has a fine oak staircase and a magnificent Delft-tiled fireplace. The upstairs room was used for illegal cock-fights (the grill for a guard to watch the stairs can still be seen). General Wolfe was born there in 1726. It was the headquarters of the York Layerthorpe Cycling Club from 1834. Today's photograph shows the timbers exposed again to good effect. The Leeds Arms (closed 1935) was next door on the corner of Haymarket; the Woolpack was over the road.

RIGHT: THE BLACK Bull Hotel. On the corner of St Sampson's Square and Finkle Street, this top-heavy tavern was one of the oldest pubs in York and also served as a music hall. You can just see a concert poster on the left of the building. The hotel was demolished in 1949 to be replaced by practical but unremarkable buildings (*see* p. 81).

(*Author's collection*)

PART OF THE new station project, the Royal Station Hotel opened in 1878 under the management of LNER. A five-storey building of yellow Scarborough brick, it featured elegant, high-ceilinged banqueting rooms and 100 large bedrooms for 14s a night. The twenty-seven-room west wing was added in 1896, named Klondyke after the US gold rush of the same year. The hotel was later renamed the Royal York. This was York's second Royal Station Hotel; the first had been next to the second station.

ABOVE: A LAD'S day out on decorated horse and charabanc leaving the Phoenix Inn in George Street, near Fishergate Bar, *c.* 1906. The pub was originally called the Labour in Vain. The modern photograph (below) shows the pub hasn't changed all that much, although the impressive lamp and adjoining terraces have gone. The pub has held regular jazz nights for some years. Dick Turpin is buried nearby.

(Courtesy of Melvyn Browne)

4

SHOPS, MARKETS AND FACTORIES

TERRY'S OF YORK, Bishopthorpe. Terry's moved to this purpose-built Baroque Revival building in 1930 from the Clementhorpe site which they had occupied since 1862. The firm was eventually bought by Kraft and the factory was closed in 2005 with the Grade II listed building and the site currently up for redevelopment. Terry's originated as confectionary manufacturers Bayldon & Berry, moving from Bootham to St Helen's Square in 1824 when Joseph Terry, an apothecary, sold his stock of drugs and joined them. By 1840, Terry's products, including candied eringo, coltsfoot rock, gum balls and lozenges made from squill, camphor and horehound, were being delivered to seventy-five towns all over England. Apart from boiled sweets, they also made marmalade, marzipan, mushroom ketchup and calves' jelly. Conversation lozenges, precursors of Love Hearts (with such slogans as 'Can you polka?', 'I want a wife', 'Do you love me?' and 'How do you flirt?'), were particularly popular. Chocolate production began around 1867, with thirteen chocolate products added to the other 380 or so confectionary and parfait lines. Up until the Second World War, 'Theatre Chocolates' were available with rustle-proof wrappers. The famous Chocolate Orange (which started life as a Chocolate Apple) was born in 1932 and, at one point, one in ten Christmas stockings reputedly contained a Terry's Chocolate Orange. In the 1990s, seven million boxes of All Gold were sold in a year.

(Courtesy of Melvyn Browne)

ABOVE: JOHN SAMPSON, bookseller and newsagent, with staff on York station forecourt. Today the building and business is occupied by W.H. Smith. The footbridge opened in 1900 (with the original bookshop at the foot of the stairs) – before that passengers had to use the subways. The platforms were given the numbers in use today in 1938.

ABOVE: PARLIAMENT STREET market seen from St Sampson's Square. This is where York's main market was held until 1955, when the gradual move to Newgate began, taking nine years to complete and shown today in the photograph below. Parliament Street is still the venue though for frequent weekend, often continental, markets. Originally the market extended from Pavement to St Sampson's Square, five rows of stalls deep.

(Courtesy of Joe Dickinson)

(Courtesy of Melvyn Browne)

ROWNTREES LEETHAM'S MILL Warehouse at Hungate. This was one of the largest flour mills in Europe. It was designed by Walter Penty in 1895 and comprised five storeys and a nine-storey water tower complete with battlements and turrets. It is surrounded on three sides by the Foss and Wormald's Cut. Spillers took it over in 1928 and Rowntrees bought it in 1937 for cocoa bean storage. It was damaged in a major fire in 1933. The main Rowntrees site was, and still is, on Haxby Road, albeit now under the ownership of Nestlé. The first part was built on 23 acres; in 1897 Rowntrees & Co. was established with working capital of £226,000 and 1,200 workers. By 1907, the company occupied 222 acres and employed around 7,000 workers.

(Courtesy of Joe Dickinson)

OPPOSITE THE EXISTING Marks & Spencer in Pavement, the Marks & Spencer Penny Bazaar opened in 1907, with the revolutionary marketing slogan: 'Don't ask the price: it's a penny'. Taken about 1914, the old photograph (above) clearly shows another retailing first: an apparent free admission policy to encourage customers to go in and browse. Pavement was called thus because around 1329 it was the only clear piece of paved land in the centre of the city. Before that it was called Marketshire as it was the site of markets (there once was a market cross there), proclamations and public punishments, in days when the punishment was made, and seen, to fit the crime: for example, drunks were made to stand on barrels with pint pots on their heads and goose thieves were put in the stocks with goose wings draped unceremoniously around their necks.

(Courtesy of Melvyn Browne)

ABOVE: AT THE top of Micklegate Hill on the left of the street, Merry's the bakers, confectioners and tea rooms shows some impressive advertising by Hovis. The building is now Micklegate post office (right). Micklegate featured open drains on each side of the street which were called the King's Ditches, and were the sole source of sanitation for many years.

ABOVE: A CHARMING shot of the top-hatted Pot Lady watching over her extensive wares at the Thursday Market (St Sampson's Square) – the origins of which date back to the fourth century. Setting up and packing up must have taken quite a while. Davygate is opposite, with Arthur's Postcard Emporium just out of shot to the left. Dawson's Banqueting Saloon and Gray's and Jowell's are now Browns department store.

(Courtesy of Melvyn Browne)

(Courtesy of Melvyn Browne)

ABOVE: A POSTCARD collector's heaven! Arthur's Postcard Emporium in Davy Hall (or Lardiner Hall) in Davygate, *c.* 1898. James W. Arthur was the pioneer of the picture postcard in York, publishing the first card depicting the city in 1893, some twenty-four years after the invention of the postcard in Austria. The legendary William Hayes had some of his photographs adapted to Arthur's cards. At one point Arthur's stock exceeded half a million cards and the firm reported in 1904 that 'The demand for postcards is still enormous; we cannot print them fast enough.' The firm sold 130 different series of postcards: these included York Arms in gold and colour (twelve cards), and Royal York (sixty-four cards), 'including Palace, Coney Street, King's Staith etc.' Back then there was some resistance to postcards from those who were uncomfortable with the thought that the servants might

read the very public messages written on them. Despite this, 575,000 cards were sold on the first day they were introduced in Britain. As can be seen, Arthur also sold violin strings. Davy Hall was demolished in 1745 to make way for New Street. Today the building is occupied by Hobbs, a ladies' clothes shop.

ABOVE: A 1913 photograph of J.B. Richardson's on Lord Mayor's Walk near Monk Bar. They provided everything equestrian for the horse and rider and did travel bag and golf bag repairs. It later became Bulmer's second-hand shop (still there on the corner) and today it is an eye-catching guitar and guitar accessory shop offering on-line as well as shop business.

(Courtesy of Melvyn Browne)

(Courtesy of Melvyn Browne)

ABOVE: PARLIAMENT STREET shops. Isaac Walton's ('high class tailors also at London and Newcastle') can be seen at Nos 39-40; opposite is Coppergate with Isaac Poad, corn and potato merchant, who also sold Yorkshire ham and bacon, turnips, mangold and clover seeds! Next door Braime's was a Tadcaster Breweries pub and Melia's was a tea store proudly calling itself the 'largest retailers in the kingdom'. The character of these old shops has been somewhat lost in the contemporary replacements.

ABOVE: YORK'S ELECTRICITY generating station, *c.* 1905. Opened in 1899, the lights first went on in York that year. The ground around the station (run by York Corporation Electricity Committee) vibrated with the noise and the 30,000hp created by the generating station. In 1929 ordinary lighting consumers (16,470 of them) paid 3½*d* per unit. The number of units sold (in millions) were: domestic: 180; public lighting: 38; industrial: 219. In 1951 this had increased as follows: domestic: 68,083, public lighting: 2,592; industrial: 76,533. The chimney has survived but all else is gone, except the ducks on the Foss.

(Courtesy of Melvyn Browne)

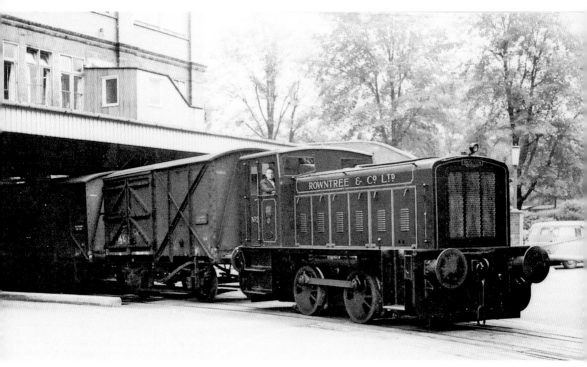

ABOVE: THIS INTERESTING photograph was taken at No.1 Landing Stage at Wigginton Road in the early 1970s. These shunters are all gone now; the modern photograph (below) shows what is now Nestlé products typically being transported by road. In 1862, Isaac Rowntree bought the Quaker Mary Tuke's grocery in Castlegate (which had been passed on to William Tuke in 1752); it specialised in tea, cocoa and chocolate. He set up the factory in Tanner's Moat. Joseph took over in 1897 with 1,000 employees, doubling by 1902 and again in 1907. During the Second World War, Rowntrees had to comply with restrictions on sugar imports, forcing them to adapt while at the same time helping the war effort: part of the office block on Haxby Road was requisitioned by the Royal Army Pay Corps. The cream department produced munitions, Ryvita and dried egg, while the gum department became a secret shell casing and fuse factory, masquerading under the name of County Industries Ltd.

(Courtesy of Melvyn Browne)

TERRY'S OF YORK packing department (below) and tower (left). The 135ft-tower had a dual purpose: as a water tower (the water coming from the nearby Ouse) and as a chimney. Note the Terry clock. On a clear day, from the top of the tower, you can see the Dales, some forty-five miles away. During the Second World War, the tower was used as an observation post watching POWs in the Knavesmire camp next door. Although production of boiled sweets continued throughout the war years (for supply to rescue ships as survival rations), F. Hills & Sons, manufacturers and repairers of aircraft propeller blades, moved into their factory from Manchester for the duration.

(Courtesy of Melvyn Browne)

(Courtesy of Joe Dickinson)

ABOVE: AN EARLY 1890s Temperance Society coffee stand in Queen Street, dissuading railway workers from mixing work with drink. You'd be forgiven for thinking that alcohol in the workplace was a thing of the distant past, but in April 2010 Carlsberg workers in Copenhagen went on strike after drinking lager was finally banned in the factory – except during lunch breaks. In 1929 there were three temperance hotels in York: The Minster Commercial in St Martin's Crescent off Micklegate; Frank's at 134 Micklegate; and Young's Private & Commercial at 24 High Petergate. In the late eighteenth century there were sixteen small brewhouses in York. The Temperance Society was set up in Bradford in 1831. Today, hot sausages provide a less intoxicating sin.

5

BAR WALLS, BARS AND CLIFFORD'S TOWER

(Courtesy of Melvyn Browne)

MONK BAR (built about 1330) with its portcullis down, 3 March 1914. Originally called Monkgate Bar, at 63ft it is the tallest of York's bars. Designed as a self-contained fortress, assailants had to cross each floor to reach the next flight of stairs, thus exposing themselves to defensive fire. The coat of arms is Plantagenet. The bar was used as a prison in the sixteenth century for recusant Catholics, and others: in 1588 Robert Walls was imprisoned for 'drawing blood in a fray'. The barbican was removed in the early 1800s. To rent the rooms at the top, one Thomas Pak (master mason at the Minster) paid 4s per annum.

(Courtesy of Joe Dickinson)

ABOVE: THE RED Tower (named after the colour of its brickwork – all the other walls and towers being built with Tadcaster limestone) can be seen behind the swings, along with the city walls bordering on Foss Islands Road. Its walls are 4ft thick. The tower was built around 1490 by Henry VII and restored in 1857 after being damaged in the Civil War siege of York. The original roof was flat and it boasted a projecting toilet. It was also known as Brimstone House because it was employed as a gunpowder warehouse; it was used as a stable around 1800. Today, the geese are still there although the swings have gone.

WALMGATE BAR, ORIGINALLY known as Walbesgate. This is the only York Bar with its barbican intact, thanks largely to William Etty RA, who campaigned tirelessly for its preservation. In 1489 it was set on fire by rebels and then bombarded during the Civil War. The inner façade dates from the sixteenth century and still retains its Doric and Ionic columns.

(Author's collection)

THE INTERIOR OF Clifford's Tower. The tower was probably named after Francis Clifford, Earl of Cumberland, who restored it for use as a garrison after it had been partly dismantled by Robert Redhead in 1592. Alternatively, its name is said to come from Roger de Clifford, whose body was hung there in chains in 1322. Originally built in wood by William the Conqueror when he visited to establish his northern headquarters in 1190, it was burnt down when 500 terrified York Jews sought sanctuary here from an anti-Semitic mob. Faced with the choice of being killed or forced baptism into the Christian faith, many committed suicide; 150 others were slaughtered. The tower was rebuilt in stone by King John and Henry III as a quadrilobate between 1245 and 1259 as a self-contained stronghold and royal residence; it housed the kingdom's Treasury in the fourteenth

century. Robert Aske, one of the prime movers in the Pilgrimage of Grace, was hanged from Clifford's Tower on 12 July 1537. On 23 April 1684, the roof was blown off during an over-enthusiastic seven-gun salute. The motte is 48ft high and the tower itself 33ft. The moat was fed by a diversion from the Ouse.

ABOVE: MICKLEGATE BAR in the 1930s, taken from Blossom Street. Micklegate Bar was originally called Mickleith, which means great gate; the royal arms are those of Edward III; the side arch was added in 1753. This was the Bar by which royal visitors entered York, it being the road to and from London. Edward IV, Richard III, Henry VII, Margaret Tudor, James I, Charles I (on three Civil War occasions) and James II all passed through. Henry VIII was scheduled to enter here but in the event came in through Walmgate Bar. Famous heads to have decorated the Bar include Lord Scrope of Mastan in 1415. The Flint and Wright shops are now the Punch Bowl, and a driving school is now on the left.

(Courtesy of Melvyn Browne)

ABOVE: THE BAR during the horse-drawn tram era, *c.* 1904. Thompson's the butchers had been taken over by the Punch Bowl pub extension by the 1930s (*see* p. 53). The Brasso advert on the horse-drawn tram and the early warning sign for the garage and motor works through the Bar give a flavour of the day – and the prevalence of children out on their own in the street. The arch is Norman, while the rest of the building dates from the fourteenth century. Heads and quarters of traitors were routinely displayed on the top, most famously: Sir Henry Percy (Hotspur) after his part in the rebellion against Elizabeth I; Richard Duke of York after the Battle of Wakefield in 1460, prompting Shakespeare to write: 'Off with his head and set it on York's gates; so York did overlook the town of York' (Queen Margaret in *Henry VI*); and Thomas Percy in 1569 – his head remained there for two years. Removal of heads without permission was aptly punishable

by beheading – guess where the heads went? The last displays were in 1746 after the Jacobite Rebellion at Culloden. The barbican was removed in 1826 to allow a circus access to the city.

ABOVE: THE BAR walls looking towards the station, *c.* 1920. The steam train going under the walls is coming from where the old station used to be. The shed on the left was built in 1845 and housed the Scarborough trains. The wall here was breached in 1839 and 1845 to give better access to the new station; the other breach opposite the Railway Offices took place in 1876. The walls were built in the thirteenth and fourteenth century on a rampart dating from the ninth and eleventh centuries. They survive for the best part of their 2-mile length, as do the four Bars and thirty-seven internal towers. Four of the six posterns and nine other towers have gone or have been rebuilt. The walls for the most part are 6ft wide and 13ft high. Burials from the 1832 cholera epidemic have been found here. The new photograph (below) shows Hudson House, built in 1969, on the right.

(Courtesy of Melvyn Browne)

ST GEORGE'S OR Fishergate Bar. More men loitering at bars (*see* p. 51 and 54). This is the gateway to Selby, taken about 1906; chains ran across the River Foss here to the castle to reinforce York's defences. The John Smith's Phoenix Inn can be seen to the right in Long Close Lane. In the 1850s the landlord was a Mr Meggeson Fields. Falconer's was a furnishers. The bar was blocked in 1489 after rebels damaged it in protest at punitive taxation (fire damage is still visible); it was eventually reopened in 1827. In Elizabethan times it was a prison for rascals and lunatics.

(Courtesy of Melvyn Browne)

6

YORK MINSTER AND OTHER PLACES OF RELIGION

(Courtesy of Melvyn Browne)

ALL SAINTS' CHURCH, North Street. Comprises Early English, Decorated and Perpendicular styles; an eight-sided tower features an unusual 120ft spire. Emma Raughton, a visionary anchorite, lived in an anchorhold here – a two-storey house attached to the aisle. The church has some of the finest medieval stained glass in Europe, including the aisle window which shows the Six Corporal Acts of Mercy (as in *Matthew*) and the famous 1410 Doom Window, which graphically depicts the last fifteen days before the Day of Judgement. There is also an outstanding fifteenth-century hammer-beam roof decorated with colourful angels. Around 1500, York had eight monasteries and friaries, over forty parish churches and two ecclesiastical colleges.

(Author's collection)

ABOVE: A VIEW of York Minster and Bootham Bar taken from the York City Art Gallery in Exhibition Square in the 1950s. To the right can be seen Bootham Bar and the de Grey Rooms (built 1841), once the Officers' Mess for the Yorkshire Hussars and a popular venue for dances before, during and immediately after the Second World War. Bootham Bar (originally Buthum which means 'at the booths' and signifies the markets which used to be held here) stands on the north-western gateway of the Roman fortress and was originally called Galmanlith. A doorknocker was added in 1501 for the use of Scotsmen seeking admission to the city. The barbican came down in 1835 and the wall steps were built in 1899; a statue of Ebrauk, the pre-Roman founder of York, once stood nearby. Thomas Mowbray's severed head was stuck here in 1405 and the Earl of Manchester bombarded the Bar in 1644 during the Civil War. In the modern photograph (below) we can see the Art Gallery fountains which replace the garden surrounding the 1911 statue of local artist William Etty (1787-1849) in the older shot. We have a lot to thank Etty for when it comes to the surviving walls, Bars and buildings of York.

(Courtesy of Melvyn Browne)

ABOVE: GREAT PETER returns, 1914. The 10.8 ton bell, Great Peter, arriving back at York Minster, presumably to be blessed before being re-hung. As can be seen, the bell was originally cast by John Taylor & Co. of Loughborough in 1840 and is Britain's second biggest bell after Great Paul – which Taylor's also cast (9ft high and weighing 17 tons) and hangs in St Paul's Cathedral. Great Peter is the heaviest of the Minster's ring of twelve bells (but, despite its weight, can be swung and rung by one person). Taylors was set up in 1784 and still trades today. The bells were restored and returned here in March 1914 by John Warner & Sons Ltd from their Spitalfields Bell Foundry. The Minster can boast thirty-five bells in total. The north-west tower contains Great Peter and six clock bells (the largest weighing 3 tons). The south-west tower houses fourteen bells (tenor is 3 tons) hung and rung for change ringing and twenty-two carillon bells (tenor 1.2 tons) which are played from a baton keyboard in the ringing chamber.

MARGARET CLITHEROW'S ORATORY in the Shambles in 1969 (above) and 2010 (below). Margaret was the wife of John Clitherow, a butcher who lived here at No. 35 (or possibly at No. 10). During Elizabeth I's persecution of Catholics, Margaret was first jailed in 1577 for not attending church. She was jailed twice more at York Castle, the second time for twenty months. Between 1582 and 1583, five priests were executed at Tyburn on Knavesmire and, when not in jail, Margaret would go at night to the gallows to visit the bodies. She was found guilty in 1586 of 'harbouring and maintaining Jesuits and priests, enemies to Her Majesty'. The usual penalty was hanging, but due to her refusal to offer a plea at her trial at the city assizes in the Guildhall she was sentenced to be pressed to death (*peine forte et dure*) by having a door weighted with nearly half a ton of boulders placed on top of her at the tollbooth on Ouse Bridge. Within fifteen minutes she was dead. She was beatified in 1929 and canonised in 1970. Her embalmed hand is said to be kept in the Bar Convent.

7

YORK PEOPLE AND SPECIAL OCCASIONS

A STATUE OF Napoleon outside a tobacconist's in Bridge Street.

(Courtesy of Joe Dickinson)

ABOVE: FARRIERS AT Fulford Cavalry Barracks, possibly attached to the Royal Dragoon Guards. Built in 1796, the barracks were initially very unpopular because horse manure was routinely piled up outside the men's windows and there were no latrines for nocturnal use. The barracks were largely demolished by the army in the 1970s. The adjacent Infantry Barracks were built between 1877 and 1880, at a cost of £15,000. In 1951 the barracks were renamed Imphal Barracks after the West Yorkshire Regiment's brave defence of Imphal Plain, Burma, in June 1944. Today it is home to HQ York Garrison, 15 (NE) Brigade HQ, 2 Signal Regiment and the Defence Vetting Agency.

ABOVE: ROAD WORKERS in 1929, possibly Irish navvies descended from families who came over fleeing the famines. In 1841 there were 327 Irish in York; in 1851 there were 1928. They tended to concentrate themselves together in areas depending on where they came from, for example Mayo and Sligo. The contemporary shot (below) shows contractors at work on the long-awaited multi-storey car park at York District Hospital, due for completion in April 2011.

(Courtesy of Joe Dickinson)

ROYAL FLYING CORPS FIRST VISIT TO YORK 21 FEB 13

(Courtesy of Joe Dickinson)

ABOVE: ROYAL FLYING Corps on Knavesmire in 1913. The dawn of aviation was a time of few suitable landing places, so the racecourse and surrounding land was an obvious choice when the army needed to land at York. Their first visit was on 21 February 1913, pictured here. After the German bombardment of Hartlepool, Scarborough and Whitby in December 1914, 33 Squadron was stationed here, causing much anger amongst local residents fearing that their presence would attract bombing raids to York. In the event, the city was bombed by Zeppelin L-21 in May 1916, one of three such raids in which nine people were killed and twenty-eight badly injured. York Races moved to the Knavesmire in 1731 from flood-prone Clifton, sometimes attracting crowds of over 100,000. The races were accompanied by side shows, gypsy bands and cock fights. They were timed to follow the assizes in August, when the gentry were in town for court business and death sentences were inevitably delivered. York's gallows had been on the Knavesmire from 1379 (Tyburn) and now public executions became a popular part of a day at the races. Part of John Carr's 1754 Grandstand can still be seen today (below).

(Courtesy of Joe Dickinson)

ABOVE: THE GRAND Yorkshire Gala. Ascents in hot air balloons were a regular feature at the annual gala, held in the grounds of Bootham Park Hospital (which became known as Gala Fields) from 1858 to 1923. One year, one of the balloons broke its moorings and took its eight passengers on an unexpected, albeit short, ride. Other attractions included military bands, roundabouts, helter-skelter (Holdsworth's Alpine Glassade – 'Why go to Switzerland?' 'Ladies Specially Invited'), evening firework displays, acrobatics, juggling and shooting galleries. It was so popular that it became a three-day event and seriously depressed attendances at York Races when it was on. The gala moved to Fulford in 1924 and then to the Knavesmire. Today's picture shows the pavilion next to the pleasant bowling green in Clarence Gardens.

(Courtesy of Melvyn Browne)

ABOVE: THE HOUSEHOLD Cavalry processing through Micklegate Bar during the visit by Queen Elizabeth II and the Duke of Edinburgh on 28 June 1971 to celebrate the 1,900th anniversary of the founding of York by Roman governor Petillius Cerialis and named Eboracum by geographer Ptolemy. The year of celebration began with a New Year's Eve Ball in the Assembly Rooms and finished with the December production of Handel's *Messiah* in the Minster. Other events included a six-day Services Searchlight Tattoo on Knavesmire in September; £1 million-worth of military hardware on display on the Knavesmire including a Thunderbird guided-missile, a Chieftain tank and a Navy Whirlwind helicopter; a Bootham Park gala with fireworks finale; an exhibition of an Edwardian fair; a 1,900th celebration evening race meeting; the Sealed Knot Re-enactment Society procession and ball; and the cremation of Emperor Severus after a torchlight procession.

ABOVE: FLOODS AT Clifton Green in 1947. The winter of 1947 was particularly long and harsh, and the floods here were a result of melting snow. The Ouse poured (with cruel appropriateness) into Water End, through Clifton Green and into Water Lane. Despite the hardship, it looks as though everyone was making the most of it, particularly the schoolboys in the boat – possibly St Peter's pupils – on their way to rescue the girls on the left. St Philip and St James Church can be seen on the right. The 1947 floods were the worst since 1831, and were almost as bad as the November 2000 flood when the Ouse was nearly 18ft above its normal level and responsible for a stretch of water larger than Lake Windermere, causing over 60,000 sandbags to be deployed.

ABOVE: THE *RIVER King* boat trip on the Ouse. A special trip to open the new water treatment plant at Acomb Landing – note the onlookers on Lendal Bridge, the band on the boat and the fine attire of the passengers. Rowntrees old factory can be seen in the background in Tanner's Moat; the factory was vacated for the Haxby Road site in 1892. The man boarding in the top hat is the chairman of York Water Company. The contemporary photograph (below) shows the *River Prince*, one of the many tourist boats, working the Ouse today.

(Courtesy of Melvyn Browne)

8

A TOUR AROUND YORK

(Courtesy of Melvyn Browne)

BRINDLEYS BUILDINGS, HUNGATE. In some areas, such as Walmgate, the infant mortality rate was one in three before the age of one – as highlighted by Seebohm Rowntree's ground-breaking *Poverty: A Study in Town Life in 1901*: researchers visited 11,500 families and found that 25 per cent of the city population was visibly poor – in 'obvious want and squalor'. The 1851 census tells us that at Britannia Yard in Walmgate 171 people shared one water pipe, one drain and four privies. In Walmgate in 1913, the death rate was twenty-three per 1,000, almost twice York's average. Using powers under the 1930 Housing Act, York Corporation began to clear the slums: streets off Walmgate and in Hungate were demolished, and residents moved to new council estates outside the city centre. At the end of 1880 there were 8,000 ash midden privies in York, some of which can be seen in this photograph. A sewerage disposal system was installed in 1890.

(Courtesy of Melvyn Browne)

HUNGATE DERIVES FROM *Hundgate*, 'street of the dogs', a common Viking street name. The image above shows a street party in Garden Street in 1907 for the Temperance Society's York Adult Schools Jubilee. Education for all was their mission. A contemporary pamphlet urges residents to 'come as you are; do not stoop to black your boots'. As a result of Rowntree's *Poverty*, in 1908 and 1914 York's medical officer, Edmund Smith, produced reports condemning streets in Hungate and Walmgate as unfit for habitation; 'The back yards in Hope Street and Albert Street and in some other quarters can only be viewed with repulsion – they are so small and fetid, and so hemmed-in by surrounding houses and other buildings ... There are no amenities; it is an absolute slum.' At the 1921 census, York's population was 84,052 with 18,608 inhabited houses (4.5 persons per dwelling). Today the area boasts some fine modern flats and houses.

(Courtesy of Joe Dickinson)

ABOVE: A VIEW of Micklegate, which was previously called Myglegate (1161) and Myklegate (1180). This is looking towards the Bar and shows the 1809 Benedictine Priory which was demolished to make way for Priory Street. The Falcon Inn at 114 was a traditional dram shop (comprising two public rooms off a central passage). Joseph Hansom (1842-1900), the architect and inventor of the cab that bears his name, was born nearby. Hansom suffered from such severe depression that he shot himself in his office on 27 May 1900. Holy Trinity Church is further down the road. Richard II visited it in 1397 and the tower collapsed in 1552. Today there are ancient stocks in the church and a memorial to Dr John Burton, historian and model for Dr Slop in Sterne's *The Life and Opinions of Tristram Shandy, Gentleman*. The modern picture shows the Priory public house, named after the old priory.

(Author's collection)

A 2½-MILE stroll gets you round York's walls – the finest surviving medieval walls in England. The old photograph(above) is remarkable because it clearly shows on the right the original Rowntrees factory in Tanner Row before their move to Haxby Road in 1892. Today, Rowntrees has been replaced by the newer of the two Aviva buildings which, unlike its earlier neighbour, merges well into the surrounding cityscape. The building on the right was Walker's Repository for Horses (built 1884), reduced in height by a half in 1965 when it became a car dealers. Patrick Nuttgens described the original building as 'an exotic red and yellow Byzantine building with ramps inside, up which the horses were led to their stalls – a kind of multi-storey horse car park'. In the older image it is surrounded by pubs and the Lendal Bridge Inn, on its left was, in turn, next door to Spinks, the typewriter shop. The toll house for Lendal Bridge (1863) can be seen in the centre of the photograph.

ABOVE: THE MERCHANT Adventurers' Hall in Fossgate, 1905. Built on the site of the original 1357 building in the fifteenth-century Great Hall and Chapel of Holy Trinity still survive, as do Mercer's records going back to the early fourteenth century, providing us with a wealth of information on trade in York at the time. The building is one of York's four surviving guildhalls for the fifty or so mercantile and craft guilds; the others are the Guildhall behind the Mansion House, Merchant Taylor's in Aldwark and St Anthony's Hall in Peaseholme Green. Typically for guildhalls it had two mutual functions: the secular trade side and the religious guild (it was originally called the Fraternal and Guild of Our Lord and the Blessed Virgin, before assuming its current name in 1581) to which commercial profits were channelled to justify the business activity and to finance the hospital which was in the undercroft.

(Courtesy of Melvyn Browne)

ABOVE: THE JUNCTION of Parliament Street and Coppergate, *c.* 1900. The George Hotel in Whip-Ma-Whop-Ma-Gate can be seen in the distance, past the ice-cream stand. In 1929, The George boasted a billiard room, stabling, a covered yard for motors and electric light. William Dove & Sons, on the corner at No. 52, were ironmongers and included amongst their wares stoves, ranges, mantels and sanitary ware. A 1929 advert tells us that 'experienced workmen sent anywhere.' The offices of the *York Herald* were to the right of Poad's (*see* p. 44).

(Courtesy of Melvyn Browne)

ABOVE: LADY PECKETT'S Yard, *c.* 1904. The yard connects Fossgate with Pavement and is named after the wife of John Peckett, a Lord Mayor of York. It was called Bacusgail (Bake House Lane) in 1312. The building on the left was an auctioneers, while Richardson's at the end of the passage was a money lender. Joseph Rowntree II rented a building in the yard to house one of his many schools. Mary Kitching was president of the 'B' class of Lady Peckett's Yard Ladies School for fourteen years, until in 1892 she left to do missionary work in the Holy Land. A lion from a circus in Parliament Street escaped and was eventually cornered here in the early 1900s.

(Author's collection)

AT THE JUNCTION of King's Court and Newgate, Pump Court was the site of one of the many water pumps and wells that served the city. Piped water was turned on in parts of the city between 1677 and 1685, and a public bath house was opened in 1691. John Wesley preached in a room ('the oven') here in 1753; it became an official place of worship for Methodists in 1754. The old painting (left) is by F. Robson and clearly shows the beautiful lantern tower window on the left – one of only two surviving in England and now sadly hidden from view to York's residents and visitors. Pump Court was originally called Pump Yard and was home to Betty Petre, who kept her cattle there before slaughter in Shambles, and Mr Huber, who collected sheep guts and washed them in a drain before exporting them to Germany to make fiddle strings. Other residents included a sweep and a prostitute, referred to locally as 'an old knock'.

(Author's collection)

LEFT: MENTIONED IN the Domesday Book, the Latin name for Shambles is *in Macello*. Along with nearby Whip-Ma-Whop-Ma-Gate, it is perhaps one of the most famous streets in the world and is the most visited street in Europe. In 2010 it won the Google Britain's Most Picturesque Street Award. Shambles was originally called Haymongergate to signify the hay that was here to feed the livestock before slaughter; after that it was called Needlergate after the needles made here from the bones of slaughtered animals. It gets its present name (at first The Great Flesh Shambles) from the fleshhammels – a shammel being the wooden board butchers used to display their meat on. They would throw their rancid meat, offal, blood and guts into the runnel in the middle of the street to add to the mess caused by chamber pot disposal from the overhanging jetties. In 1280, seventeen butchers paid an annual shammel toll of 70s between them; in 1872, twenty-five out of the thirty-nine shops here were butcher's, out of a total of eighty-eight in the whole of York; two butcher's: C.W. Mee (on the right) and J.W. Collier (on the left) can be seen here. There were also four pubs: The Globe (closed 1936); the Eagle & Child (closed 1925); the Neptune (closed 1903) and the Shoulder of Mutton (closed 1898). The street is narrow by design, to keep the sun off the meat.

ABOVE: A VIEW of Jubbergate, which was originally called Joubrettagate (the 'Street of the Bretons' in the Jewish Quarter) and Jubretgate. On the left is Webster's kitchen and bath-ware shop, which became Pawson's, specialists in rubber-ware. An advert from 1929 tells us what's for sale there: Mackintoshes, overshoes, cycle covers, hot water bottles, etc. You can see the tin baths on display outside the shop. Little Shambles is to the right; the building at the end was A. Wells, a broker's, around 1880; then the White Rose Inn (as here); then Forrington's furnishers, around 1920; and

now Gert & Henry's restaurant. At one stage in its life it was home to six families. Jubbergate originally extended to cover what is today Market Street as far as Coney Street. York's first police station is on the left and F. Orrington – furniture shop and repairer's – had perambulators for hire. Butcher's F. Robinson are on the right with Dalby's boot store on the left. Today the street is on the edge of the bustling Newgate market.

(Courtesy of Joe Dickinson)

CONEY STREET. THE earliest record of the name is in 1213, when it was called Cuningstreta, from the Viking words *konungra* 'king' and *straet* 'street'. So, it was, and is, King's Street. Below is a 1950s photograph looking towards St Helen's Square. Leak & Thorp's is on the left on the site of the fourteenth-century Old George Inn, demolished in 1869; Charlotte and Anne Brontë stayed there in 1849. The fine clock outside St Martin le Grand Church dates from 1668; it was damaged in the Baedeker Raid but restored in 1966 (complete with the naval figure with sextant who survived the raid) and it is still telling us the time today. The church is now a moving shrine to all those who lost their lives in the two world wars. The magnificent Great West Window (31ft high and 13ft wide) was prudently removed at the beginning of the Second World War and is now in the south aisle. Margaret Clitherow was married there two years before converting to Roman Catholicism. On the far right is Archibald Ramsden's piano and organ shop, which had moved from St Sampson's Square. Next door to Leak & Thorp was the Black Boy Chocolate Kabin, which was later sold to Maynard's.

(Author's collection)

(Courtesy of Joe Dickinson)

BROWNS CORNER IN St Sampson's Square. The square was a slave market in late Roman times. The building seen above was occupied by D. Lofthouse fruit and potato merchants on the ground floor with Archibald Ramsden, piano and organ shop on the first floor. Dawson's shaving rooms was next door and is now Browns department store. Founded by Henry Rhodes Brown in 1891, it has been here since 1900. Davygate, to the left, is named after David le Lardiner (clerk of the kitchen). His job was to stock the king's larder; in the twelfth century David's father, John, was the royal lardiner for the Forest of Galtres – a title which became hereditary – David received land from King Stephen in 1135. Davygate was the site of the forest courthouse prison.

MUCKY PEG LANE, off St Sampson's Square. Now Finkle Street, the lane was a notorious haunt for prostitutes – which presumably accounts for the name. The pub is the Black Bull, demolished in the 1960s. On the right is the Roman Bath pub (formerly the Mail Coach), where you can see part of the Roman bathhouse excavated in 1930 (parts of the cold room (frigidarium), hot room (caldarium) and underfloor central heating system (hypocaust) are on display). Other snickelways of ill repute were Penny Lane and Straker's Passage off Fossgate. Mad Alice Lane, between Swinegate and Low Petergate, is named after Alice Smith, who was hanged for the crime of insanity in 1825 (*see* p. 32).

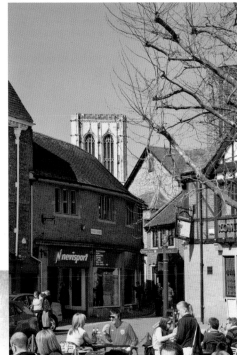

(Author's collection)

(Author's collection)

TWO VIEWS OF Low Petergate, looking towards High
Petergate and the Minster. Scott's the pork butchers
can be seen on the left (closed in 2009) as can Seale's
Brush and Mat Warehouse 'Dealer in Small-Wares'
– the huge brush hanging on the outside is now in
the Castle Museum. Sir Thomas Herbert (Charles
I's secretary, who was with him at his execution)
lived here. The Little Brass Shop is halfway down
on the right. Misses Pearson Ye Olde Parkin Shoppe
was at Nos 27-28 'old fashioned confectioners' and
specialists in 'Yorkshire Parkin – packed and posted
to any address'. The Landsboro Arms is on the
right next to Merriman's pawnbrokers. Guy Fawkes
was born just off Low Petergate, was baptised at St
Michael-le-Belfry and was a pupil at St Peter's.

(Author's collection)

ABOVE: MANSION HOUSE in the 1960s. Mansion House is the official residence of the Lord Mayor during his or her year in office. York had a house for its Lord Mayor even before London; it was built between 1723 and 1733 on the site of the chapel of the Guild of St Christopher. It houses the York Civic Plate and Insignia – notably the sword of the Emperor Sigismund, which originally hung over his stall as Knight of the Garter in St George's Chapel, Windsor and was given to York in 1439. Sigismund was King of Hungary and Croatia from 1387 to 1437, and Holy Roman Emperor from 1433 until 1437. A Terry's van can be seen on the right outside the shop and restaurant in this picture. Betty's neo-Georgian building, fitted out by Ward & Leckenby, is prominent in the modern photograph (below). The Square was purchased from St Helen's churchyard in 1703 to allow the gentry carriage access to the Assembly Rooms in nearby Blake Street. The Mansion House is famously threatened with being burnt to the ground in Gaskell's *Sylvia's Lovers* (1863) if the Mayor, in 1777, failed to satisfy the demands of the press-gang.

(Author's collection)

ABOVE: AN IDEALISED 'chocolate box' picture of Terry's Restaurant in St Helen's Square, taken from ... a box of Terry's All Gold chocolates. The first-floor café-restaurant and ballroom and ground-floor shop were as famous in their time as Betty's (directly opposite in the square) is now. Items on the menu in 1900 included: Russian tea (6*d*); Scotch Woodcock (1*s*); Harum Scarum (2*s*) and Gentleman's Relish Sandwich (1*s*). In 1924, Harker's Hotel (then opposite) opposed the renewal of Terry's music licence on the grounds that the music and dancing was keeping guests awake and making the owner ill. Terry's counsel submitted at one point that 'jazz might not be music but a very large number of people like it'. The licence was renewed on condition that Terry's kept the windows closed. The restaurant closed in 1980 and is now a jeweller's, although the Terry's name lives on under the windows and between the Corinthian pillars.

RIGHT: STONEGATE IN the 1950s. By common consent, Stonegate is one of the finest streets in England, if not Europe, and York's first 'foot-street', pedestrianised in 1971 and paving the way for many more. You can clearly see the gallows sign of Ye Olde Starre Inne stretching across the street – originally erected in 1792 by landlord Thomas Bulmer who was obliged to pay the owner of the building over the street on to which it joined 5s rent per year. In 1886 it read 'Boddy's Star Inn'; the pub is named after Charles I – popularly known as 'the Old Star'. Stonegate was once famous for its coffee shops (hence Coffee Yard). Mulberry Hall – the timber-framed building on the right – was built in 1434 and was then Lorimer's fishmongers; today it is a china shop. Next

(Author's collection)

door, on the right, was Bellerby's Public Library. The old Roman paving survives under the cobbles, complete with the central gulley for the chariots' skid wheels. The shop on the near right is Stonegate Silk Shop. Queen Mary, wife of George V and living at Goldsborough Hall near Knaresborough, was a frequent shopper here in the 1920s and '30s: unfortunately for the shop owners she was a devotee of 'honouring' – a practice whereby patronage alone was considered sufficient payment for the goods with which she left the shops.

(Courtesy of Rupert Matthews)

VOLANS HOTEL, DUNCOME Place, in what is now the extension to the late Gothic Dean Court Hotel with St Wilfrid's Roman Catholic Church (1864) on the left. Originally the building was occupied by a homeopathic dispenser who moved to Stonegate in 1807. Duncombe Place was named after Dean Augustus Duncombe in 1858, who himself subscribed £1,000 to help finance the building of the Place, which involved the demolition of Lop Lane (Flea Alley) in 1834.

BELOW: A 1906 photograph showing the Assembly Rooms (one of the earliest neo-classical buildings in Europe – now a pizza restaurant) in Blake Street and, over the road, the fine sweep of the late Georgian council terrace. It originally contained seven houses, a library and the Yorkshire Club. The Assembly Rooms were built in 1732 in the Palladian style and paid for by subscription to provide the local gentry with somewhere sumptuous to play dice and cards, dance and drink tea, as featured in Smollett's *The Expedition of Humphrey Clinker*. The building epitomised the age of elegance and helped make York the capital of north country fashion. The main hall is surrounded by forty-eight Corinthian pillars. The building on the right is the Red House, which was built in 1718 on the site of St Leonard's Hospital and which has recently been restored; the candle snuffer is still to the right of the door. It was once the home of Dr John Burton (Shandy's Dr Slop) and it is now an antiques centre. Burton was a gynaecologist and writer; his books included *An Essay Towards a Complete System of Midwifery*, illustrated by no less an artist than George Stubbs, who had come to York (then, as now, a centre of excellence in medical science) to learn his anatomy. He ended up teaching medical students before moving on to perfecting his comparative anatomy and painting his famous horse paintings. His most celebrated, Whistlejacket, was painted in 1762 and featured the very same horse that won the four-mile chase for 2,000 guineas at York in August 1759.

(Courtesy of Melvyn Browne)

ABOVE: A 1908 view of the elegant street that is Bootham (originally Galman, which extended from Bootham Bar to Marygate) looking towards the Minster and showing the house (No. 49) once lived in by Joseph Rowntree in the middle left. Called Lady Armstrong's Mansion and bought for £4,500, it included 6 acres of land and was later taken over by Bootham School. Opposite was W.H. Auden's house.

(Courtesy of Melvyn Browne)

(Courtesy of Melvyn Browne)

THE JUNCTION OF Gillygate, Clarence Street and Lord Mayor's Walk (above and right, top). The house on the right was a doctors' surgery (Drs Platt and Golden in the 1950s) where the 2009 York St John University extension building now is. The university originally opened in May 1841 as a college with principal, masters and one student and two campuses. It was initially called York and Ripon Diocesan Training School for Masters and, after the closure of the Ripon campus in 2006, became the university it is today. Clarence Street houses and nearby Union Street car park were built on land in 1835 called the Horsefair; three horse fairs were held here every year. Gillygate (right, below) was originally called Invico Sancti Egidi, then Giligate in 1373 after St Giles' Church. The church was demolished in 1547; the Salvation Army citadel, opened by General Booth in 1882, now stands on the site.

89

LORD MAYOR'S WALK, opposite the walls and the Minster. Stanley's Winter Nips – the pocket doctor – on the side wall of Richardson's the butchers has since been replaced by the iconic Nightly Bile Beans Keeps You Healthy, Bright-Eyed & Slim advertisement still there today. York's second university, York St John University, occupies most of the rest of the road. In 1916, halfway through the First World War, St John's College (as it was then) had to close because all the male students had gone to the Front. The building was requisitioned as a military hospital until it re-opened in 1919. The affiliated women's college in Ripon stayed open, though, so that the female students could make clothes, bandages and splints for the soldiers at the Front. In 1718, trees were planted down the middle of Lord Mayor's Walk – an early bid to improve the environment here.

(Courtesy of Melvyn Browne)

OUR LADY'S ROW and
Goodramgate (above and right,
top). Goodramgate is named
after Guthrum, a Danish chief
active around AD 878. The Grade
I listed Lady's Row cottages
(Nos 60-72) pictured here date
from 1316. They are the oldest
surviving jettied cottages in
Britain. Originally nine or ten
houses, the one at the southern
end was demolished in 1766
to make way for a gateway to
Holy Trinity Church. They
each comprised one 10ft
by 15ft room on each floor.
Rents collected went to pay for
chantries to the Blessed Virgin
Mary in nearby churches.
Sanderson's Temperance
Hotel can be seen opposite the
cottages in the first building on
the right of the street. Two pubs
occupied the cottages at various
times: The Hawk's Crest (from
1796-1819) and the Noah's
Ark (around 1878).

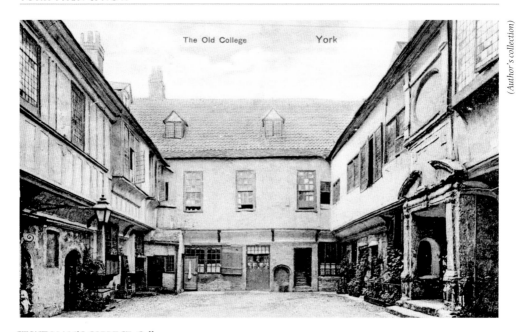

(Author's collection)

The Old College   York

ST WILLIAM'S COLLEGE, College Street. Originally the House of the Prior of Hexham, it is named after William Fitzherbert, great-grandson of William the Conqueror and Archbishop of York from 1141. He was disgraced and sacked in 1148 but reinstated on appeal (*see* p. 21). St William's embalmed head (he died in suspicious circumstances in 1154 – a poisoned chalice?) was preserved in York Minster. The above photograph, taken in about 1890, shows the fifteenth-century half-timbering covered in stucco; it was removed again in 1906. The college was split into tenements at the time but was formerly home to the Minster's Chantry, twenty-three priests and their provost. They had been indulging in 'colourful nocturnal habits' and were billeted in the nearby college so that their behaviour could be monitored more closely. One incident involved one of the cathedral freelances in an argument in Minster Gates hitting a man over the head with the blunt end of an axe. College Street was originally called Little Alice Lane and then Vicar Lane.

ST WILLIAM'S COLLEGE and Minster Chapter House. Charles I established his propaganda printing house here during the Civil War and it was used as the Royal Mint at one time. The current central doors were made by Robert Thompson of Kilburn. His trademark mouse can be seen on the right-hand door. A rental document of 1845 tells us that annual rents are 32s for five tenements, three cottages (2s each) and one messuage (2s 4d). From 1680 to 1761 the cottages were variously occupied by a painter, joiner, translator and cordwainer. They were nearly demolished in 1912 to make way for the tramline to Heworth. Appropriately, the cottages are now the Minster's Visitor Centre, brass rubbing centre and restaurant. George Hudson had a draper's store in one of the shops here.

(Courtesy of Joe Dickinson)

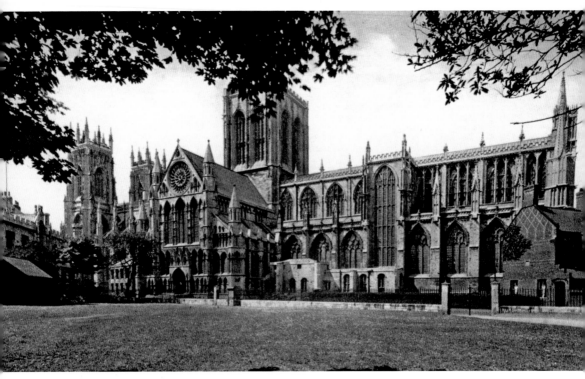

THE EMPEROR CONSTANTINE (left) outside the Minster (above). Constantine the Great was the only Roman emperor to be proclaimed Augustus while in Britain, in 306; he converted to Christianity in a ceremony outside the Minster after seeing a vision of the cross when consulting his Roman gods before a battle. York thereby became a vital centre of early Christianity. A marble head of Constantine was found during an excavation in Stonegate. From 1750 the South Door of the Minster here boasted a fine clock above the arch; this was removed in 1871 and put in its present position in 1883 in the North Transept, complete with the two men who strike the four quarters, salvaged from a Middle Ages predecessor.

(Author's collection)

(Author's collection)

BELOW: ROWNTREES WORKERS starting or finishing their shift by foot, bicycle or bus on Haxby Road bridge. The number 27 bus ran between Haxby Road, St Leonards and the station. The famous clock is still there today. Until 1951 Haxby Road was known as Peppermill Lane, after the peppercorn windmill opposite Fountayne Street, owned by the Randerson family. During the First World War, Rowntrees' dining block was converted into a military hospital for casualties returning from the Front.

Other local titles published by The History Press

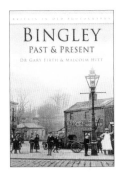

Bingley Past & Present
DR GARY FIRTH & MALCOLM HITT

This fascinating book takes a nostalgic look back at Bingley and presents some of the changes that have taken place in the town during the last 150 years. Local authors Dr Gary Firth and Malcolm Hitt have gathered together ninety pairs of images, many previously unpublished, to compare and contrast changing modes of fashion and transport, shops and businesses, houses and public buildings, whilst recalling the people who once lived and worked in this historic market town.

978 0 7524 5345 3

Haunted York
RUPERT MATTHEWS

Haunted York contains a chilling collection of true-life tales from around the city. From the medieval stonemasons who haunt York Minster to a reincarnation mystery at St Mary's Church, the spectres of King's Manor, Micklegate Bar and Exhibition Square and the many spirits found in the city's public houses, this phenomenal gathering of ghostly goings on will delight everyone interested in the paranormal.

978 0 7524 4910 4

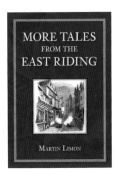

More Tales from the East Riding
MARTIN LIMON

Yorkshire's old East Riding has had a rich and varied past, and Martin Limon's second collection of historical stories is filled with more of the remarkable people, places and events that have made it that way. This volume contains tales of the East Riding's most famous residents, including William Wilberforce and Amy Johnson, alongside some forgotten aspects of the region's past – including the crime that shocked eighteenth-century Long Riston and health care in the area before the arrival of the NHS.

978 0 7524 4753 7

Blind Jack of Knaresborough
ARNOLD KELLETT

Jack Metcalf was blinded by smallpox at the age of six, but he did not let this stop him from leading an astonishing and adventurous life – becoming an expert horseman, gambler and guide. He eloped at the age of twenty-one, ran numerous enterprises, joined the military as a musician, and led the Yorkshire Blues onto the battlefield at Culloden.

978 0 7524 4658 5

Visit our website and discover thousands of other History Press books.

www.thehistorypress.co.uk